The Silly Little Book

of

WICKED JOKES

The Silly Little Book
of
WICKED JOKES

This is a Parragon Book

This edition published in 2002

Parragon
Queen Street House
4 Queen Street
Bath BA1 1HE, UK

Produced by Magpie Books, an imprint of
Robinson Publishing Ltd, London

Copyright © Parragon 1999

ISBN 0-75257-905-3

A copy of the British Library Cataloguing-in-Publication Data
is available from the British Library

Printed and bound in Singapore

Contents

WICKED SLIMIES   1

WICKED GUYS AND GALS   55

WICKED WITCHES   89

WICKED WILD ANIMALS   127

WICKED SPOOKS   153

WICKED LESSONS   179

WICKED WISECRACKS   205

THAT'S WICKED   230

Wicked Slimies

Worms – where's the fun in spending your entire existence burrowing through muck? Get a life!

What did one slug say to another who had hit him and rushed off? I'll get you next slime!

How do you know your kitchen is filthy?
The slugs leave trails on the floor that read "Clean me."

What did the slug say as he slipped down the window very fast?
How slime flies!

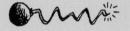

What's the difference between
school dinners and a pile of slugs?
School dinners come on a plate.

What do you do when two snails
have a fight?
Leave them to slug it out.

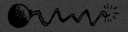

How did the clever snail carry his
home?
He used a snail-trailer.

What did the cowboy maggot say
when he went into the saloon bar?
Gimme a slug of whiskey.

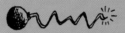

Why didn't the two worms go into
Noah's ark in an apple?
Because everyone had to go in
pairs.

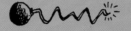

What do worms leave round their bathtubs?
The scum of the earth.

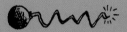

How do you make a glow-worm happy?
Cut off its tail. It'll be de-lighted.

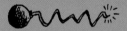

How can you tell which end of a worm is its head?
Tickle its middle and see which end smiles.

What do you get if you cross a
worm with a young goat?
A dirty kid.

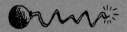

What do you get if you cross a
glow-worm with a pint of beer?
Light ale.

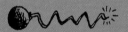

Why was the glow-worm unhappy?
Because her children were not very
bright.

What did the woodworm say to the chair?
It's been nice gnawing you!

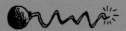

What did one maggot say to the other who was stuck in an apple?
Worm your way out of that one, then!

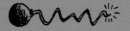

One worm said to the other "I love you, I love you, I love you."
"Don't be stupid," the other worm said, "I'm your other end!"

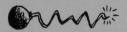

Why are glow-worms good to carry in your bag?
They can lighten your load.

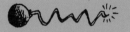

What is the worms' favorite band?
Mud.

What makes a glow-worm glow?
A light meal.

What's the maggot army called?
The apple corps.

What did one worm say to another
when he was late home?
Why in earth are you late?

What do you get if you cross a
worm with an elephant?
Big holes in your garden.

What is the best advice to give a
worm?
Sleep late.

Who was wet and slippery and
invaded England?
William the Conger.

What is wet and slippery and likes
Latin American music?
A conga eel.

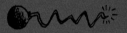

What do you get if you cross a
snake with a Lego set?
A boa constructor.

What is a snake's favorite food?
Hiss fingers.

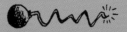

Why do babies like cobras?
Because they come with their own
rattle.

Why wouldn't the snake go on the
"speak-your-weight" machine?
He had his own scales.

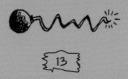

What do you get if you cross an anaconda with a glow-worm?
A thirty-foot strip light.

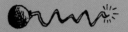

What do snakes write on the bottom of their letters?
"With love and hisses."

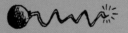

What did the snake say when he was offered a piece of cheese for dinner?
"Thank you, I'll just have a slither."

What's another word for a python?
A mega-bite.

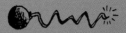

What do you get if you cross a
serpent and a trumpet?
A snake in the brass.

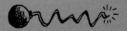

What is the difference between a
poisonous snake and a
headmaster?
You can make a pet out of the
snake.

Which hand would you use to grab
a poisonous snake?
Your enemy's.

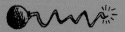

What do you do if you find a black
mamba in your toilet?
Wait until he's finished.

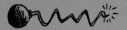

What is a snake's favorite opera?
Wriggletto.

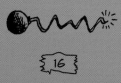

Why did the two boa constrictors
get married?
Because they had a crush on each
other.

What should you do if you find a
snake in your bed?
Sleep in the wardrobe.

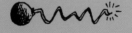

What snakes are good at sums?
Adders.

What do you get if you cross a
snake with a hotdog?
A fangfurter.

What is a snake's favorite dance?
Snake rattle and roll.

What do you get if you cross a
snake with a pig?
A boar constrictor.

What did one snake say to
another?
Hiss off!

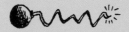

Why are snake's hard to fool?
They have no leg to pull.

What is the python's favorite pop group?
Squeeze.

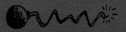

What is the snakes' favorite TV program?
Monty Python.

What do you get if you cross a bag of snakes with a cupboard of food?
Snakes and Larders.

What do you call a python with a
great bedside manner?
A snake charmer.

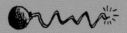

Why did the viper want to become
a python?
He got the coiling.

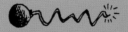

What do most people do when they
see a python?
They re-coil.

What school subject are snakes
best at?
Hiss-tory.

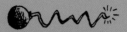

What did the snake say to the
cornered rat?
"Hiss is the end of the line mate!"

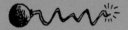

What do you call a snake who
works for the government?
A civil serpent.

What's the best thing about
deadly snakes?
They've got poisonality.

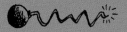

What's the snakes' favorite
dance?
The mamba.

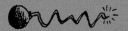

What is a snake's favorite game?
Snakes and Ladders.

What song to snakes like to sing?
Viva Aspana.

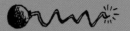

What do you get if you cross two
snakes with a magic spell?
Addercadabra and abradacobra.

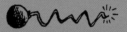

Why didn't the viper, viper nose?
Because the adder adder
handkerchief.

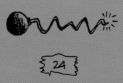

What did one snake say when the other snake asked him the time? "Don't asp me!"

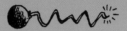

What do you give a sick snake? Asp-rin.

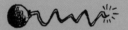

What kind of letters did the snake get from his admirers? Fang mail.

Which snakes are found on cars?
Windscreen vipers.

What do you get if you cross a
serpent and a trumpet?
A snake in the brass.

What's the definition of a nervous
breakdown?
A chameleon on a tartan rug.

What kind of tiles can't you stick
on the wall?
Rep-tiles.

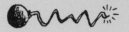

What do you call a rich frog?
A gold-blooded reptile.

How do frogs manage to lay so
many eggs?
They sit eggsaminations.

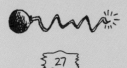

What kind of bull doesn't have horns?
A bullfrog.

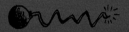

What jumps up and down in front of a car?
Froglights.

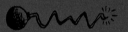

What did the frog use to cross the road?
The green cross toad.

When is a car like a frog?
When it's being toad.

What did the bus conductor say to the frog?
Hop on.

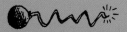

What do you get if you cross a frog with a ferry?
A hoppercraft.

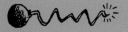

What do you call a frog who wants to be a cowboy?
Hoppalong Cassidy.

Why do frogs have webbed feet?
To stamp out forest fires.

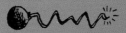

What is a frog's favorite dance?
The Lindy Hop.

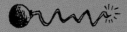

What do frogs sit on?
Toadstools.

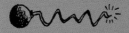

What would you get if you crossed
a frog with a little dog?
A croaker spaniel.

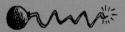

How do frogs die?
They Kermit suicide.

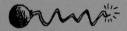

Why doesn't Kermit like
elephants?
They always want to play leap-frog
with him.

What is a frog's favorite game?
Croak-et.

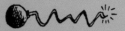

What is a frog's favorite flower?
The croakus.

What do you get if you cross a
planet with a toad?
Star warts.

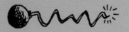

Where do you get frogs eggs?
In a spawn shop.

There was an old man called Jake
Who had a poisonous snake
It bit his head
And now he's dead
So that was the end of Jake.

A boa with coils uneven
Had the greatest trouble in
breathing
With jokes she was afflicted
For her laughs got constricted
And her coils started writing and
wreathing.

A cobra was invited to dine
By his charmingly cute valentine
But when he got there
He found that the fare
Was pineapple dumplings with
wine.

1st person: I've just been bitten by a snake on one arm.
2nd person: Which one?
1st person I don't know, one snake looks very much like the next one.

Mother: John, why did you put a slug in auntie's bed?
John: Because I couldn't find a snake.

1st man: My wife eats like a bird.
2nd man: You mean she hardly
eats a thing?
1st man: No, she eats slugs and
worms.

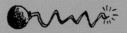

1st snake: I'm glad I'm not
poisonous!
2nd snake: Why?
1st snake: Because I've just bitten
my tongue.

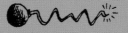

Fisherman: What are you fishing
for sonny?
Boy: I'm not fishing, I'm drowning
worms.

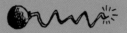

Boy: I once met a lion who had
been bitten by a snake.
Girl: What did he say?
Boy: Nothing, silly, lions don't talk!

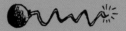

Surveyor: This house is a ruin. I wonder what stops it from falling down.
Owner: I think the woodworm are holding hands.

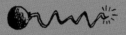

Boy: What's black, slimy, with hairy legs and eyes on stalks?
Mom: Eat the biscuits and don't worry what's in the tin.

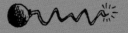

Did you hear about the stupid woodworm?
He was found in a brick.

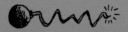

Did you hear about the maggot that was shut up in Tutankhamun's tomb?
It had a phar-old time.

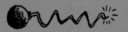

Did you hear about the woodworm who stopped doing his work?
He said it was boring.

Doctor, doctor, I think I'm turning
into a frog.
Oh, you're just playing too much
croquet.

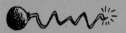

Doctor, I keep thinking I'm a
python.
Oh you can't get round me like
that, you know.

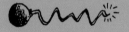

Doctor, doctor, I keep thinking I'm an adder.
Oh good, could you help me with my tax return?

Doctor, doctor, I keep thinking I'm a toad.
Go on, hop it!

Doctor, doctor, I keep thinking I'm a snail.
Don't worry, we'll soon have you out of your shell.

Doctor, doctor, I keep thinking I'm a woodworm.
How boring.

Doctor, doctor, I keep thinking I'm a snake about to shed its skin.
Just slip into something more comfortable.

Waiter, waiter! There's a slug in my salad.
I'm sorry, sir, I didn't know you were a vegetarian.

Waiter, waiter! There's a slug in my dinner.
Don't worry, sir, there's no extra charge.

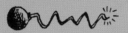

Waiter, waiter! There's a slug in my lettuce.
Sorry madam, no pets allowed here.

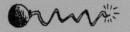

Waiter, waiter! There's a worm in my soup.
That's not a worm, sir, that's your sausage.

Waiter, waiter! There are two worms on my plate.

Those are your sausages, sir.

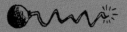

Waiter, waiter! Have you got frogs legs?

No, sir, I always walk like this.

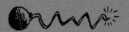

Waiter, waiter, are there snails on the menu?

Oh yes, sir, they must have escaped from the kitchen.

Waiter, waiter! I can't eat this meat,
it's crawling with maggots.
Quick, run to the other end of the
table, you can catch it as it goes
by.

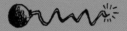

Waiter, waiter! There's a slug in my
lettuce.
Quiet, they'll all want one.

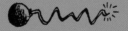

Waiter, waiter! There's a frog in my soup.
Don't worry, madam, there's not enough there to drown him.

A snake went into a café and ordered a cup of tea. "That will be $2," said the waitress, "and may I say that it's nice to see you here. We don't get many snakes coming in here." "I'm not surprised at $2 for a cup of tea!" he replied.

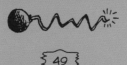

A frog walked into a library and asked the librarian what he would recommend. "How about this, sir?" asked the librarian, showing him *Toad of Toad Hall*. "Reddit, reddit," said the frog.

A woman walked into a pet shop and said, "I'd like a frog for my son."
"Sorry madam," said the shopkeeper, "we don't do part exchange."

What did the witch say to the ugly toad?
"I'd put a curse on you – but somebody beat me to it!"

What is a snail?
A slug with a crash helmet.

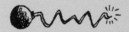

Spook: Should you eat spiders and slugs and zombie slime on an empty stomach?
Witch: No, you should eat them on a plate.

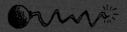

Witch: I'd like a new frog, please.
Pet Shop Assistant: But you bought one only yesterday. What happened?
Witch: It Kermit-ted suicide.

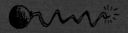

Did you hear about the snake with a bad cold?
No! Tell me about the snake with a bad cold.
It had to viper nose.

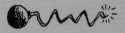

Did you hear about the scientist who crossed a parrot with a crocodile?
It bit off his arm and said, "Who's a pretty boy then?"

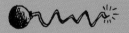

What's a crocodile's favorite
game?
Swallow my leader.

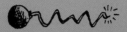

Dad, do slugs taste nice?
Of course not, why do you ask?
Because you've just eaten one
that was in your salad.

Wicked Guys
and Gals

What do you call an insect from
outer space?
Bug Rogers.

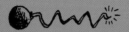

What do you get if you cross the
Lone Ranger with an insect?
The Masked-quito.

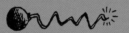

What powerful reptile is found in
the Sydney Opera House?
The Lizard of Oz.

What do you call a frog who wants
to be a cowboy?
Hoppalong Cassidy.

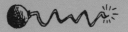

What do you get if you cross a
toad with a mist?
Kermit the Fog.

Who has large antlers, has a high
voice and wears white gloves?
Mickey Moose.

What is Dr Jekyll's favorite game?
Hyde and Seek.

Did you know that Dr Jekyll has
created a new medicine?
One sip and you're a new man.

Why did the witch keep turning
people into Mickey Mouse?
She was having Disney spells.

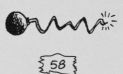

What do you get if you cross
Dracula with Al Capone?
A fangster.

What is the vampire's favorite
breakfast cereal?
Ready Neck.

What's a vampire's favorite cartoon
character?
Batman.

What is green and sooty and
whistles when it rubs its back legs
together?
Chimney Cricket.

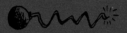

What do you get if you cross a flea
with a rabbit?
A bug's bunny.

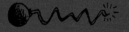

Two fleas were sitting on Robinson
Crusoe's back. One hopped off
saying "Byee! See you on Friday!"

Why was Baron Frankenstein never lonely?
Because he was good at making fiends.

What do Paddington Bear and
Winnie the Pooh pack for their
holidays?
The bear essentials.

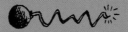

What's large and green and sits in
a corner on its own all day?
The Incredible Sulk.

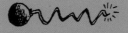

Little Miss Muffet sat on a tuffet
Eating a bowl of stew
Along came a spider
And sat down beside her.
Guess what?
She ate him up too!

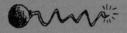

What do you get if a huge hairy
monster steps on Batman and
Robin?
Flatman and Ribbon.

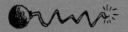

What did ET's mother say to him when he got home?
Where on Earth have you been?

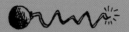

Why does the Hound of the Baskervilles turn round and round before he lies down for the night? Because he's the watchdog and he has to wind himself up.

Did you hear about the monster who was known as Captain Kirk? He had a left ear, a right ear and a final front ear.

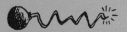

Why did J.R. see his lawyer? Because he wanted to Sue Ellen.

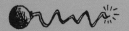

What does Rudolph the Red-Nosed Reindeer say before he tells a joke? "This one will sleigh you!"

The wonderful Wizard of Oz
Retired from business becoz
What with up-to-date science
To most of his clients
He wasn't the wiz that he woz.

Which ghost sailed the seven seas
looking for rubbish and blubber?
The ghost of BinBag the Whaler.

Superman climbed to the top of a high mountain in the middle of the African jungle. As he reached the summit he found himself suddenly surrounded by dozens of vicious vampires, ghosts, monsters and goblins. What did he say?
"Boy, am I in the wrong joke!"

Who carries a sack and bites people?
Santa Jaws.

Who is Wyatt Burp?
The sheriff with the repeater.

If King Kong went to Hong Kong to
play ping-pong and died, what
would they put on his coffin?
A lid.

Where does Tarzan buy his
clothes?
At a jungle sale.

What lives in a pod and is a Kung
Fu expert?
Bruce Pea.

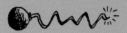

What's big, hairy and can fly?
King Koncorde.

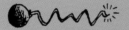

What illness did everyone on the
Enterprise catch?
Chicken Spocks.

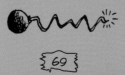

What does Luke Skywalker shave with?
A laser blade.

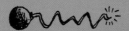

Who is in cowboy films and is always broke?
Skint Eastwood.

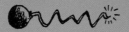

Why did Mickey Mouse take a trip to outer space?
He wanted to find Pluto.

How did Benjamin Franklin
discover electricity?
It came to him in a flash.

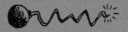

What's the difference between
Noah's Ark and Joan of Arc?
One was made of wood and the
other was Maid of Orleans.

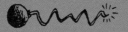

Who conquered half the world,
laying eggs along the way?
Attila the Hen.

Why was Cleopatra so
cantankerous?
She was Queen of Denial.

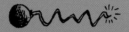

"Who's been eating my porridge?"
squeaked Baby Bear.
"Who's been eating my porridge?"
cried Mother Bear.
"Burp!" said Father Bear.

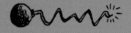

Who was the first underwater spy?
James Pond.

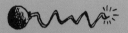

Fan: I've always admired you. Are
your teeth your own?
Actor: Whose do you think they are?

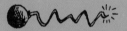

Did you hear about the film star
who had so many facelifts that
when she went for the next one
they had to lower her body
instead?

What was purple and ruled the world?
Alexander the Grape.

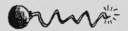

Which was the smallest plum?
Tom Plum.

Why wouldn't the ripe peach sit on the wall?
It had heard what happened to Humpty Dumpty.

Who led 10,000 pigs up a hill and
back again?
The Grand Old Duke of Pork.

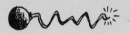

What happened to the pig who
studied Shakespeare?
He ended up in Hamlet.

What was Noah's job?
Preserving pears.

What is Dracula's favorite pet?
A Bloodhound.

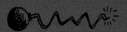

How do Daleks deal with eggs?
They eggs-terminate them.

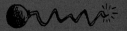

Jane: I can trace my heritage all
the way back to royalty.
Jill: King Kong?

What were Tarzan's last words?
"Who greased that vine?"

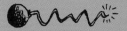

What was King Arthur's favorite game?
Knights and crosses.

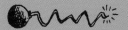

Why did King Henry VIII have so many wives?
He liked to chop and change.

What do you call a top pop group
made up of nits?
The Lice Girls.

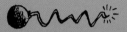

What's the grasshoppers' favorite
band?
Buddy Holly and the Crickets.

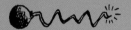

What is the insects' favorite pop
group?
The Beatles.

Who is the worms' Prime Minister?
Maggot Thatcher.

Which ghost was President of
France?
Charles de Ghoul.

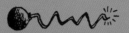

Which skeleton wore a kilt?
Boney Prince Charlie.

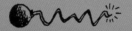

What do you call the famous
eighteenth-century skeleton who
was cremated?
Bone-ash (Beau Nash . . . geddit?)

Wizard: You have the face of a saint.
Witch: Really? Which one?
Wizard: A Saint Bernard.

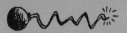

Teacher: What did Robert the Bruce do after watching the spider climbing up and down?
Pupil: He went and invented the yo-yo.

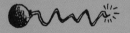

Who is the most royal ant?
Princess Ant.

Who was the most famous French ant?
Napoleant.

Who was the most famous scientist ant?
Albert Antstein.

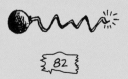

A man came home from work one day to find a ghostly figure with lots of wild hair, a long, ragged jacket and big staring eyes. "Who are you?" asked the man.

"I am the ghost of Beethoven," said the apparition.

"I don't believe you," said the man. "If you are Beethoven, perform his last movement."

"All right," said the ghost and fell off the piano stool.

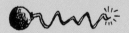

Two friends were discussing the latest scandalous revelations about a Hollywood actress. They say she likes her latest husband so much she's decided to keep him for another month, said one to the other.

Doctor, doctor, I think I'm Napoleon. How long have you felt like this? Ever since Waterloo.

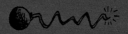

Nicky and Vicky were talking about a famous, very glamorous film star.
"What do you think of her clothes?" asked Nicky.
"I'd say they were chosen to bring out the bust in her," replied Vicky.

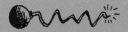

What did the cannibal say when he met the famous explorer?
Dr Livingstone, I consume?

What did Hannibal say when he saw the elephants coming? "Here come the gooseberries" – he was color-blind.

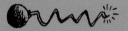

What's yellow and sings?
Banana Mouskouri.

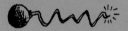

What's short and green and goes camping?
A boy sprout.

How did they divide the Roman
Empire?
With a pair of Caesers.

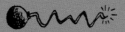

Who wrote Great Eggspectations?
Charles Chickens.

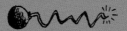

What do you get if you cross a pop
singer with a shark?
Boy Jaws.

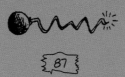

A fan approached a famous tennis player. "May I have your autograph, please?" she asked. The tennis player was in a hurry, so he said, "I don't really play tennis, you know." "I know," said the fan. "But I'd like your autograph anyway."

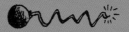

Has success gone to his head? "I don't know, but it's certainly gone to his mouth!"

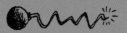

Wicked Witches

Why aren't we getting any sun
then?
Because she can't spell "sunny."

What did one witch say to the
other when they came out of the
cinema?
"Do you want to walk home or shall
we take the broom?"

What's a witch's favorite book?
Broom at the Top.

What's the witches' favorite pop
group?
Broomski Beat.

Why did the witch join Tottenham
Hotspur Football Club?
She heard they needed a new
sweeper.

What makes more noise than an
angry witch?
Two angry witches.

What do little witches like to play
at school?
Bat's cradle.

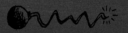

What happened to the witch with
an upside-down nose?
Every time she sneezed her hat
blew off.

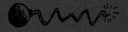

What happened when the baby
witch was born?
It was so ugly its parents ran away
from home.

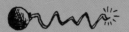

What happened when the witch
went for a job as a TV presenter?
The producer said she had the
perfect face for radio.

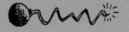

What kind of music do witches
play on the piano?
Hag-time.

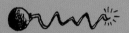

What is old and ugly and can see
just as well from both ends?
A witch with a blindfold.

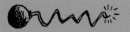

What do witches eat for
breakfast?
Rice Krispies because they snap at
them.

What do witches eat for dinner?
Real toad in the hole.

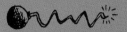

What is the best way of stopping
infection from witch bites?
Don't bite any witches.

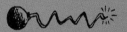

What should you expect if you drop
in on a witch's home unexpectedly?
Pot luck.

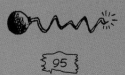

What does a witch do if her broom
is stolen?
She calls the Flying Squad.

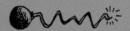

What do you call a witch who
climbs up walls?
Ivy.

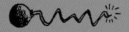

Where do the cleanest witches
live?
Bath.

What do you call a witch with one leg?
Eileen.

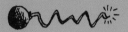

How can you tell if a witch has a glass eye?
When it comes out in conversation.

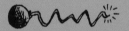

What goes "cackle, cackle, bonk?"
A witch laughing her head off.

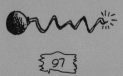

What is the witch's motto?
We came, we saw, we conjured.

How can you make a witch itch?
Take away her "W."

How does a witch tell the time?
With her witch watch.

What are little witches good at at
school?
Spelling.

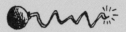

How does a witch-doctor ask a girl
to polka with him?
Voodoo like to dance with me?

What do you call a nervous witch?
A twitch.

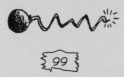

Who's the fastest witch?
The one that rides on a vroooooom
stick.

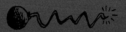

Why do witches fly on broomsticks?
Because vacuum cleaners are too
heavy.

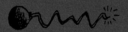

What do you get if you cross a
sorceress with a millionaire.
A very witch person.

What kind of tests do they give in
witch school?
Hex-aminations.

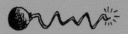

How do witches on broomsticks
drink their tea?
Out of flying saucers.

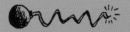

Where does a witch keep her
purse?
In a hag bag.

What do witches ring for in a hotel?
B-room service.

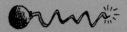

What kind of jewelry do warty witches wear on their wrists?
Charm bracelets.

What happens if you are confronted with two identical hags?
You can't tell witch is witch.

How do you know that you're in bed with a witch?
She has a big "W" embroidered on her pajamas.

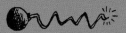

When should you feed witch's milk to a baby?
When it's a baby witch.

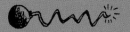

What is a little witch after she is one year old?
A two-year-old witch.

What do you call a witch who
drives really badly?
A road hag.

What is another term for a witch?
A hag lady.

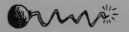

What do you call a witch who is
made of cotton and has lots of
holes in her?
A string hag.

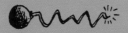

Why should men be careful of beautiful witches?
They'll sweep them off their feet.

Is it true that a witch won't hurt you if you run away from her?
It all depends on how fast you run!

What do you call a witch who kills her mother and father?
An orphan.

Why do some witches eat raw meat?
Because they don't know how to cook.

How do you make a witch float?
Take two scoops of ice cream, a glass of Coke and one witch.

What type of boats do witches sail?
Cat-amarans.

What's yellow and very poisonous?
Witch-infested custard.

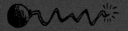

Why did the witch buy two tickets
to the zoo?
One to get in and one to get out.

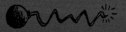

What do baby witches play with?
Deady bears.

How can you tell when witches are carrying a time bomb?
You can hear their brooms tick!

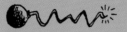

How do warty witches keep their hair out of place?
With scare spray.

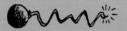

Why is "s" the witches' favorite letter?
Because it turns cream into scream.

What do you call a pretty and
friendly witch?
A failure.

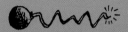

Why are witches' fingernails never
more than eleven inches long?
Because if they were twelve inches
they'd be a foot.

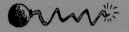

What do you call a witch who flies
in Concorde?
Lucky.

What is evil and ugly, puts spells on people and is made of leaves?
A witch (the leaves were just a plant).

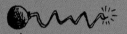

What do you do with a blue witch?
Try to cheer her up.

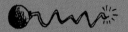

What does a witch turn into when the lights go out?
The dark.

Why do witches go to the docks?
To see the bats being launched.

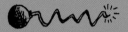

What do you do if a witch in a
pointy hat sits in front of you in the
cinema?
Miss most of the film.

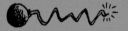

How is a witch's face like a million
dollars?
It's all green and wrinkly.

What's evil and ugly and goes up
and down all day?
A witch in a lift.

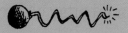

Why did the witches go on strike?
Because they wanted sweeping
reforms.

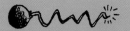

What do you call a which who likes
the beach but is scared of the
water?
A chicken sand-witch.

Who went into a witch's den and came out alive?
The witch.

What do you call two witches who share a broomstick?
Broom-mates.

What do witches use pencil sharpeners for?
To keep their hats pointed.

What is evil, ugly and keeps the neighbors awake?
A witch with a drumkit.

Why do witches have stiff joints?
They get broomatism.

Why did the witch ride on a French duster?
She felt like a dust-up.

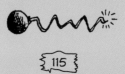

When a witch falls into a pond
what is the first thing that she
does?
Gets wet.

What would you say if you saw nine
witches in black capes flying south
and one witch in a red cape flying
north?
That nine out of ten witches wear
black capes.

Are you getting sick of witch jokes?
Then cancel your subscription to witch.

What do you call it when a witch's cat falls off her broomstick?
A catastrophe.

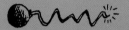

What do you get if you cross a witch's cat with Father Christmas?
Santa Claws.

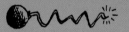

How do you get milk from a witch's cat?
Steal her saucer.

What do witches' cats like for breakfast?
Mice Krispies.

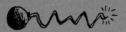

What do you get if you cross a witch's cat with a canary?
A peeping tom.

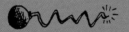

Why did the witch feed her cat with dimes?
She wanted to put them in the kitty.

What does a witch enjoy cooking most?
Gnomelettes.

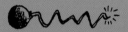

Why is a witch's kitten like an unhealed wound?
Both are a little pussy.

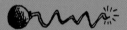

What do you call a witch's cat that drinks vinegar?
A sour puss.

What do you call a witch's cat who never comes when she's called?
Im-puss-able.

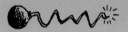

What has four legs, a tail, whiskers and flies?
A dead witch's cat.

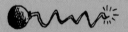

What do you get if you cross a witch's cat and a canary?
A cat with a full tummy.

1st boy: Are you having a party for your birthday?
2nd boy: No, I'm having a witch do.
1st boy: What's a witch do?
2nd boy: She flies around on a broomstick casting spells.

1st witch: I spend hours in front of the mirror admiring my beauty. Do you think that's vanity?
2nd witch: No, it's imagination.

Witch: I have the face of a 16-year-old girl.
Wizard: Well you'd better give it back, you're making it all wrinkly.

1st witch: What's your new boyfriend like?
2nd witch: He's mean, nasty, ugly, smelly, and totally evil – but he has some bad points too.

1st witch: I went to the beauty parlor yesterday. I was there for three hours.

2nd witch: Oh, what did you have done?

1st witch: Nothing, I was just going in for an estimate.

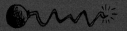

1st witch: I'm going to France tomorrow.

2nd witch: Are you going by broom?

1st witch: No, by hoovercraft.

Witch: You should keep control of your little boy. He just bit me on the ankle.

Vampire: That's only because he couldn't reach your neck.

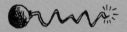

1st witch: Have you tried one of these new paper cauldrons?

2nd witch: Yes.

1st witch: Did it work?

2nd witch: No, it was tearable.

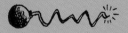

1st witch: Shall I buy black or blue candles?

2nd witch: Which one burns longer?

1st witch: Neither, they both burn shorter.

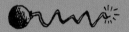

A gang of witches broke into a blood bank last night and stole a thousand pints of blood. Police are still hunting for the clots.

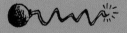

Wicked Wild Animals

Why do polar bears like bald men?
Because they have a great, white,
bear place.

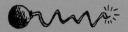

What do you get if you cross an
octopus with a skunk?
An octopong.

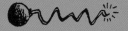

What do you get if you cross a bee
with a skunk?
A creature that stinks and stings.

What's the difference between a very old, shaggy yeti and a dead bee?
One's a seedy beast and the other's a deceased bee.

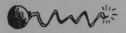

What kind of money do yetis use?
Iced lolly.

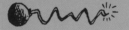

What exams do yetis take?
Snow levels.

What do you get if you cross a giant, hairy monster with a penguin?
I don't know but it's a very tight-fitting dinner suit.

What happened to the cannibal lion?
He had to swallow his pride.

What was the name of the film
about a killer lion that swam
underwater?
"Claws."

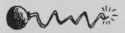

Why don't anteaters get sick?
Because they're full of anty-
bodies!

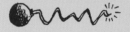

What do you get it you cross a
hedgehog with a giraffe?
A long-necked toothbrush.

What's a porcupine's favorite food?
Prickled onions.

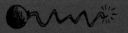

What's black and white and makes
a lot of noise?
A zebra with a set of drums.

What should you do if you find a gorilla sitting at your school desk? Sit somewhere else.

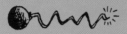

What did the stupid ghost call his pet tiger?
Spot.

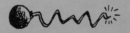

Why was the mother kangaroo cross with her children?
Because they ate crisps in bed.

What's the difference between a coyote and a flea?
One howls on the prairie, and the other prowls on the hairy.

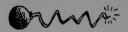

Have you ever seen a man-eating tiger?
No, but in the café next door I once saw a man eating chicken!

A group of Chinamen who were on safari in Africa came across a pride of lions. "Oh look," said one of the lions. "A Chinese takeaway."

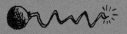

1st lion: Every time I eat, I feel sick.
2nd lion: I know. It's hard to keep a good man down.

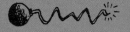

The eighth Earl of Jerry was showing Americans round his ancestral home, Jerry Hall, when one of them pointed to a moth-eaten, stuffed polar bear. "Gee! That beast sure smells," said the American. "Why d'ya keep it?" "For sentimental reasons. It was shot by my mother when she and my father were on a trip to the Arctic."

"What's it stuffed with?" asked the American.

"The seventh Earl of Jerry!"

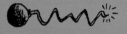

What's the difference between a gooseberry, a gorilla, and a tube of glue?
I don't know.
Well, you can bite into a gooseberry, but you can't bite into a gorilla.
What about the tube of glue?
I thought that was where you'd get stuck!

What's green and wobbly and hangs from trees?
Giraffe snot.

What's an alligator's favorite
game?
Snap.

Why shouldn't you play cards in
the jungle?
There are too many cheetahs.

What do you get if you cross an
OXO cube with a hyena?
A laughing stock.

What do you get if you cross a
giraffe with a hedgehog?
A hair brush with a very long
handle.

Why did King Kong want to join the army?
Because he wanted to study gorilla warfare.

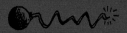

We had roast boar for dinner last night.
Was it a wild boar?
Well, it wasn't very pleased.

Teacher: Now, today, we're going to study the wildlife of Africa, starting with elephants. Now pay attention and look at me or you may never know what an elephant looks like!

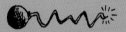

Where do you find wild yetis?
It depends where you left them.

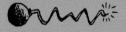

What's the difference between a
wild camel and a bully?
One's a big, smelly, bad-tempered
beast and the other is an animal.

What do you get if you cross a dog
with a lion?
A terrified mailman.

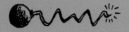

The great Roman emperor Caesar was watching Christians being thrown to the lions. "One good thing about this sport," he said to one of his aides, "we're never bothered with spectators running onto the pitch."

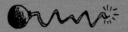

A question in Sam's biology exam asked him to name ten animals that were found in Africa. Sam wrote down, "Nine elephants and a lion."

Did you hear about the boy who was told to do 100 lines?
He drew 100 cats on the paper. He thought the teacher had said lions.

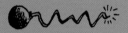

In the park this morning I was surrounded by lions.
Lions! In the park?
Yes – dandelions!

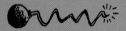

Pa was taking Danny around the museum when they came across a magnificent stuffed lion in a glass case. "Pa," asked the puzzled Danny, "how did they shoot the lion without breaking the glass?"

On which side does the tiger have most of his stripes?
On the outside.

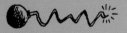

What's worse than a giraffe with a sore throat?
A centipede with chilblains.

Some vampires went to see Dracula.
They said, "Drac, we want to open a zoo. Have you got any advice?"
"Yes," replied Dracula, "have lots of giraffes."

What did the cowboy say when the bear ate Lassie?
Well, doggone!

What animal do you look like when you get into the bath?
A little bear.

Why shouldn't you take a bear to the zoo?
Because they'd rather go to the cinema.

What should you call a bald teddy?
Fred bear.

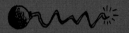

What's got two humps and
changes color?
A camel-ion.

What is a bear's favorite drink?
Koka-Koala.

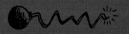

What do you get if you cross a
skunk with a bear.
Winnie the Pooh.

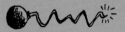

Have you ever hunted bear?
No, but I've been shooting in my
shorts.

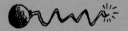

What do you get if you cross a
teddy bear with a pig?
A teddy boar.

Why do bears have fur coats?
Because they'd look stupid in
anoraks.

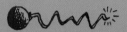

What's a teddy bear's favorite
pasta?
Tagliateddy.

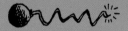

How do you hire a teddy bear?
Put him on stilts.

Why was the little bear so spoiled?
Because its mother panda'd to its
every whim.

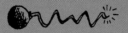

Teddy: If you were walking through
a Canadian forest and you met a
bear, would you keep on walking or
turn round and run?
Eddie: I'd turn round and run.
Teddy: What, with a bear behind?

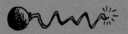

Why do bears wear fur coats?
They'd look silly in plastic macs.

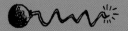

How do you start a teddy bear
race?
Say, ready, teddy, go!"

Wicked Spooks

Why did Frankenstein squeeze his girlfriend to death?
He had a crush on her.

What did Dr Frankenstein get when he put his goldfish's brain in the body of his dog?
I don't know, but it is great at chasing submarines.

Why did Frankenstein's monster give up boxing?
He was worried he might spoil his looks.

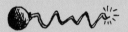

What happened to Frankenstein's monster on the road?
He was stopped for speeding, fined $50 and dismantled for six months.

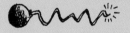

Dr Frankenstein: Igor, have you seen my latest invention? It's a new pill consisting of 50 per cent glue and 50 per cent aspirin.
Igor: But what's it for?
Dr Frankenstein: For monsters with splitting headaches.

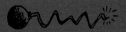

What did Frankenstein's monster say when he was struck by lightning?
Thanks, I needed that.

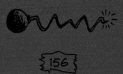

What should you do if you find
yourself surrounded by Dracula,
Frankenstein, a zombie and a
werewolf?
Hope you're at a fancy dress party.

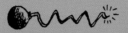

What did one of Frankenstein's
ears say to the other?
I didn't know we were living on the
same block.

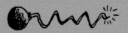

Igor: Only this morning Dr Frankenstein completed another amazing operation. He crossed an ostrich with a centipede.

Dracula: And what did he get?

Igor: We don't know – we haven't managed to catch it yet.

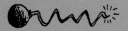

Igor: How was that science fiction movie you saw last night?

Dr Frankenstein: Oh, the same old story – boy meets girl, boy loses girl, boy builds new girl . . .

Dr Frankenstein: I've just invented something that everyone in the world will want! You know how you get a nasty ring around the bathtub every time you use it, and you have to clean the ring off?
Igor: Yes, I hate it.
Dr Frankenstein: Well you need never have a bathtub ring again! I've invented the square tub . . .

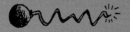

What happened when Dr Frankenstein swallowed some uranium?
He got atomic ache.

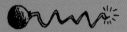

Dracula: Have you seen the new monster from Poland?
Frankenstein: A Pole?
Dracula: Yes – you can tell from his wooden expression.

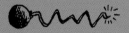

Frankenstein: Help, I've got a short circuit!
Igor: Don't worry, I'll lengthen it.

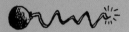

Igor: Dr Frankenstein's just invented a new kind of glue.
Dracula: I hope it doesn't make him stuck up.

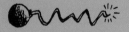

Monster: Someone told me Dr Frankenstein invented the safety match.

Igor: Yes, that was one of his most striking achievements.

What is written on the grave of Frankenstein's monster?

Rust in Peace.

How do you join the Dracula Fan
Club?
Send you name, address and
blood group.

Did you hear about Dr
Frankenstein's invention for
cooking breakfast?
He crossed a chicken with an
electric organ and now he's got
Hammond eggs.

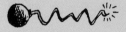

What is a ghost's favorite TV program?
Horrornation Street.

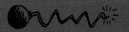

When Annie first went to school she was puzzled by people talking about the Chamber of Horrors. "What do you mean?" she asked nervously.
"It's what we call the staff room," explained her friend.

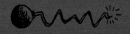

What's the only kind of dog you can eat?
A hot dog.

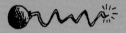

If a wizard were knocked out by Dracula in a fight what would he be?
Out for the Count.

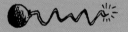

Why does Dracula have no friends?
Because he's a pain in the neck.

What's Dracula's favorite dance?
The fang-dango.

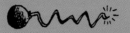

What did Dracula say to the
Wolfman?
You look like you're going to the
dogs.

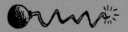

What do you get if you cross
Dracula with Al Capone?
A fangster.

Why did Dracula go to the dentist?
He had fang decay.

What does Dracula say when you
tell him a new fact?
Well, fangcy that!

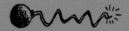

Why was Dracula thought as being
polite?
He always said fangs.

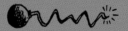

Did you know that Dracula wants
to become a comedian?
He's looking for a crypt writer.

What do you get if you cross
Dracula with Sir Lancelot?
A bite in shining armour.

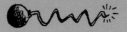

What does Mrs Dracula say to Mr
Dracula when he leaves for work in
the evening?
Have a nice bite!

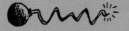

What's Dracula's car called?
A mobile blood unit.

What kind of medicine does
Dracula take for a cold?
Coffin medicine.

Where is Dracula's American
office?
The Vampire State Building.

What did Dracula say to his new apprentice?
We could do with some new blood around here.

What did Dracula call his daughter?
Bloody Mary.

Two teenage boys were talking in the classroom. One said, "I took my girlfriend to see *The Bride of Dracula* last night."

"Oh yeh," said the other, "what was she like?"

"Well she was about six foot six, white as a ghost and she had big red staring eyes and fangs."

The other said, "Yes, but what was the Bride of Dracula like?"

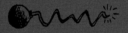

What is Dracula's favorite
pudding?
Leeches and scream.

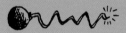

Which old song did Dracula hate?
Peg O' My Heart.

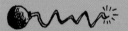

Why did Dracula miss lunch?
Because he didn't fancy the stake.

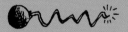

What's the name of Dracula's cook?
Fangy Craddock.

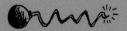

Why does Dracula live in a coffin?
Because the rent is low.

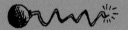

When he's out driving, where does Dracula like to stop and eat?
The Happy Biter.

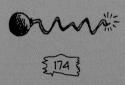

What is Dracula's motto?
The morgue the merrier.

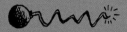

What sort of ship does Count
Dracula sail on?
A blood vessel.

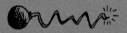

How does Dracula keep fit?
He plays batminton.

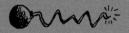

What's Dracula's favorite society?
The Consumer's Association.

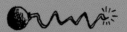

What is Count Dracula's favorite
snack?
A fangfurter.

Was Dracula ever married?
No, he was a bat-chelor.

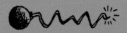

Why was Dracula always willing to help young vampires?
Because he liked to see new blood in the business.

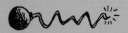

Why is Dracula a good person to take out to dinner?
Because he eats necks to nothing.

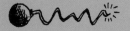

What do you call a dog owned by Dracula?
A blood hound.

What do you get if you cross a
midget with Dracula?
A vampire that sucks blood from
your kneecaps.

Why is Dracula so unpopular?
'Cos he's a pain in the neck.

What do you think of Dracula
films?
Fangtastic!

Wicked Lessons

The school once went on an outing by train to the seaside, and the journey hadn't been progressing for very long when the teacher rushed up to the conductor and said, "Stop the train! Stop the train! One of the children has just fallen off!"

"That's all right," he replied calmly. "They'd all paid for their tickets."

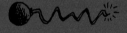

The class was on a field study trip in the countryside. "What a pretty cow that is," said Annie.

"That's a Jersey," said her teacher.

"Really?" asked Annie. "I thought it was her skin."

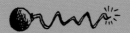

Peter: Every Wednesday afternoon our teacher takes us out and we go for a tramp in the woods.

Anita: That sounds nice. Does the class enjoy it?

Peter: Yes, but the tramp's getting a bit fed up.

"Did you enjoy the school outing?"
asked Mother.
"Oh, yes," said Jemima. "And we're
going again tomorrow."
"Really?" asked Mother.
"Whatever for?"
"To look for the children who got
left behind."

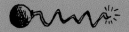

What did the school wit say as the
class boarded the boat?
Every time I go on a ferry it makes
me cross.

On the train coming home Davy asked the teacher, "What was the name of that station we just stopped at?"

"I didn't notice," replied the teacher. "I was reading. Why do you ask?"

"I thought you'd like to know where Eddie and Freddie got off."

Johnny was asked if he could spell Mississippi.

He replied, "Well, I can start, but I'm not sure when to stop."

Deirdre: I wish we could go somewhere really wild and remote on our school trip.
Dora: Why?
Deirdre: I want to go where the hand of man has never set foot.

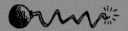

One year the school went to the Natural History Museum in London. "Did you enjoy it?" asked a teacher on the way home.
"Oh yes," replied the class. "But it was a bit funny going to a dead zoo."

Mrs Broadbeam: Now, remember, children, travel is very good for you. It broadens the mind.

Sarah, muttering: If you're anything to go by, that's not all it broadens!

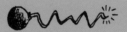

A teacher took her class for a walk in the country, and Susie found a grass snake. "Come quickly, miss," she called, "here's a tail without a body!"

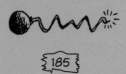

Naughty Nova nipped out one break time to visit the local shop. She asked, "Have you any broken biscuits?"

"Yes," replied the shopkeeper.

"Then you shouldn't be so clumsy," said Nova cheekily.

What happened when the wizard turned a naughty schoolboy into a hare?

He's still rabbiting on about it.

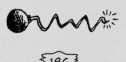

Why did the wizard turn the naughty schoolgirl into a mouse? Because she ratted on him.

Teacher: Don't shuffle your feet when you walk into assembly. Pick them up.
Naughty Nigel: When we've picked them up, are we supposed to carry them in our pockets?

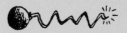

Why did the teacher keep naughty
Nigel in after school?
Because she believed that
detention was better than cure.

A girl who was at a very expensive
school turned up on her parents'
doorstep one night, very
distressed. "Daddy," she sobbed.
"I's just been expelled . . ."
"Hell's Bells!" exploded her father.
"$5,000 a term and she still says
'I's'."

Why was the little bird expelled
from school?
She was always playing practical
yolks.

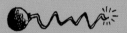

What happened to the baby
chicken that misbehaved at
school?
It was eggspelled.

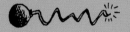

When is an English teacher like a judge?
When she hands out long sentences.

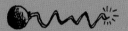

Tracy: Would you punish someone for something they haven't done?
Teacher: Of course not.
Tracy: Oh good, because I haven't done my homework.

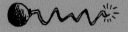

Arthur: It's true that there is a connection between television and violence.

Martha: What makes you think that?

Arthur: Because I told my teacher I had watched television instead of doing my homework, and she hit me.

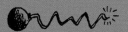

Teacher: Write "I must not forget my gym kit" 100 times.

Nicky: But, sir, I only forgot it once.

Teacher: I told you to write this poem out 20 times because your handwriting is so bad.
Girl: I'm sorry, miss – my arithmetic's not that good either.

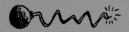

Angry Teacher: I thought I told you to stand at the end of the line!
Kevin: I did, sir, but there was someone there already!"

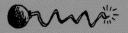

"Boys, boys!" cried the teacher, discovering yet another scrap going on. "Didn't I tell you not to fight? You must learn to give and take!"

"That's what he did," sniffed Jerry. "He took my football and gave me a black eye!"

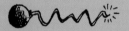

What do little witches like to play at school?
Bat's cradle.

What do little zombies play?
Corpses and Robbers.

"Why are you tearing up your homework notebook and scattering the pieces around the playground?" a furious teacher asked one of her pupils.
"To keep the elephants away, miss."
"There are no elephants."
"Shows how effective it is then, doesn't it?"

The schoolteacher was furious when Alec knocked him down with his new bicycle in the playground. "Don't you know how to ride that yet?" he roared.

"Oh yes!" shouted Alec over his shoulder. "It's the bell I can't work yet."

I smother school dinner with lots of honey.
I've done it all my life.
It makes the food taste funny.
But the peas stay on my knife.

The English teacher was trying to explain what the word "collision" meant. "What would happen," she asked, "if two boys ran into each other in the playground?"
"They'd fight," answered the class.

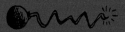

What do you get if you cross old potatoes with lumpy mince?
School dinners.

Mr Anderson, the science teacher, was very absent-minded. One day he brought a box into the classroom and said, "I've got a frog and a toad in here. When I get them out we'll look at the differences." He put his hand into the box and pulled out two sandwiches. "Oh dear!" he said. "I could have sworn I'd just had my lunch."

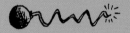

Rich boy to dinner lady: This bread's horrible. Why can't you make your own bread like the servants do at home?

Dinner lady: Because we don't have the kind of dough that your father makes!

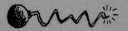

A warning to any young sinner:
Be you fat or perhaps even thinner,
If you do not repent,
To Hell you'll be sent,
With nothing to eat but school dinner.

"I have decided to abolish all corporal punishment at this school," said the principal at morning assembly. "That means that there will be no physical punishment."

"Does that mean that you're stopping school dinners as well, sir?"

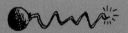

Some people say the school cook's cooking is out of this world. Most pupils wish it were out of their stomachs.

Teacher: Eat up your roast beef, it's full of iron.
Dottie: No wonder it's so tough.

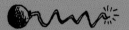

Billy: I thought there was a choice for dinner today.
Dinner lady: There is.
Billy: No, there isn't. There's only cheese pie.
Dinner lady: You can choose to eat it or leave it.

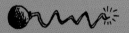

What did the children do when
there were rock cakes for lunch?
Took their pick.

What did the dinner lady say when
the teacher told her off for putting
her finger in his soup?
It's all right, it isn't hot.

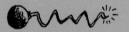

What do Scottish toads play?
Hopscotch.

Harry: Please may I have another pear, miss?

Teacher: Another, Harry? They don't grow on trees, you know.

How can you save school dumplings from drowning?
Put them in gravy boats.

Why did Rupert eat six school dinners?
He wanted to be a big success.

"Any complaints?" asked the teacher during school dinner.

"Yes, sir," said one bold lad, "these peas are awfully hard, sir."

The master dipped a spoon into the peas on the boy's plate and tasted them. "They seem soft enough to me," he declared.

"Yes, they are now, I've been chewing them for the last half-hour."

Paddy: Would you say the kids at your school are tough?
Maddie: Tough? Even the teachers play truant!

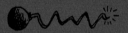

Will and Gill were comparing school meals with their mothers' cooking. "My mom's not that good a cook," said Gill, "but at least her gravy moves about on the plate."

Wicked
Wisecracks

Avril: Sometimes I really like you.
April: When's that?
Avril: When you're not yourself.

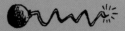

Charlie: Do you think I'm intelligent?
Chrissie: I'd like to say "yes" but my mom says I must always tell the truth.

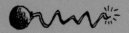

Emma: I'd like to say something nice about you, as it's your birthday.
Gemma: Why don't you?
Emma: Because I can't think of a single thing to say!

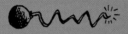

What did the builder say when he saw his non-too-bright assistant laying the lawn at a new house? "Green on top!"

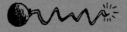

Ivan: They say Ian has a dual personality.
Ivor: Let's hope the other one is brighter than this one!

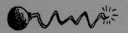

Madge: Your body's quite well organized.
Martin: How do you mean?
Madge: The weakest part – your brain – is protected by the strongest – your thick skull!

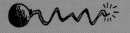

Nellie: I have an open mind.
KellyY: Yes, there's nothing in it.

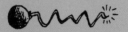

Reg: I keep talking to myself.
Roger: I'm not surprised – no one else would listen to you!

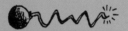

Zoe: I'm sure I'm right.
Chloe: You're as right as rain – all wet!

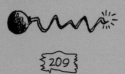

Jane: Do you ever do any gardening?
Wayne: Not often. Why?
Jane: You look as if you could do with some remedial weeding.

Holly: Do you ever find life boring?
Dolly: I didn't until I met you.

Why is your brother always flying off the handle?
Because he's got a screw loose.

You might find my sister a bit dull until you get to know her. When you do you'll discover she's a real bore!

His speech started at 2 p.m. sharp. And finished at 3 p.m. dull.

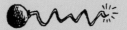

They call him Baby-face. Does that mean he's got a brain to match?

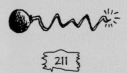

They say many doctors have examined her brain – but they can't find anything in it.

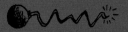

Don't let your mind wander. It's not strong enough to be allowed out on its own.

Does she have something on her mind?
Only if she's got a hat on.

First explorer: There's one thing about Jenkinson.
Second explorer: What's that?
First explorer: He could go to headhunters' country without any fear – they'd have no interest in him.

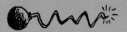

Brian: Let's play a game of wits.
Diane: No, let's play something you can play too.

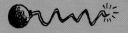

Jane: Do you like me?
Wayne: As girls go, you're fine.
And the sooner you go the better!

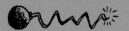

Handsome Harry: Every time I walk
past a girl she sighs.
Wisecracking William: With relief!

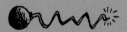

Freda: Boys whisper they love me.
Fred: Well, they wouldn't admit it
out loud, would they?

Laura: Whenever I go to the corner shop the shopkeeper shakes my hand.
Lionel: I expect it's to make sure you don't put it in his till.

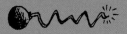

Jerry: Is that a new perfume I smell?
Kerry: It is, and you do!

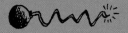

Fenton: You'll just have to give me credit.
Benton: Well, I'm certainly not giving you cash!

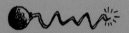

The problem is, his facial features don't seem to understand the importance of being part of a team.

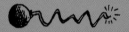

I think she's quite old, don't you?
She's got so many wrinkles on her
forehead she has to screw on her
hat.

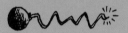

Why do you say he's got tennis-
match eyes?
He's so cross-eyed he can watch
both ends of the court without
moving his head.

She's not very fat, is she?
No, she's got a really feminine
look.
Her sister's skinny, too.
Yes, if she drinks tomato juice she
looks like a thermometer.

My girlfriend loves nature.
That's very good of her,
considering what nature has done
for her!

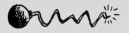

Jenny: Do you like my new suit? I'm told it fits like a glove.
Lenny: Yes, it sticks out in five places.

Gorging Gordon was so large he could sit round the table all by himself.

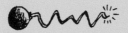

She's so poisonous that if a dog bit her it would die.

He's so cold-blooded that if a mosquito bit him it would get pneumonia.

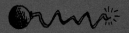

She's so ugly that even spiders run away when they see her.

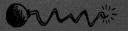

His death won't be listed under "Obituaries," it will be under "Neighborhood Improvements."

I hear she's a business woman.
Yes, her nose is always in other
people's business.

I hear they call him Caterpillar.
Why's that?
He got where he is by crawling.

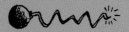

Pattie: I'd like a dress to match my eyes.
Mattie: Is it possible to buy a bloodshot dress?

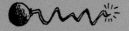

My boyfriend only has two faults – everything he says and everything he does!

He thinks everyone worships the ground he crawled out of.

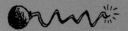

I hear she doesn't care for a man's company.
Not unless he owns it.

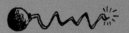

I hear he's a very careful person.
Well, he likes to economize on soap and water.

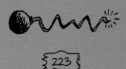

Doesn't he look distinguished?
He'd look better if he were
extinguished.

I hear he has a quick mind.
Yes, he's a real scheme engine.

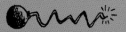

Owen: Thank you so much for
lending me that money. I shall be
everlastingly in your debt.
Lenny: That's what I'm afraid of!

Ronnie: I can trace my family tree way back.
Bonnie: Yes, back to the time you lived in it!

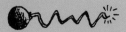

They say she has a sharp tongue.
Yes, she can slice bread with it.

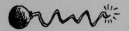

Does he tell lies?
Let's just say his memory exaggerates.

Jane: I'll cook dinner. What would you like?
Shane: Good life insurance.

They say he's going places. The sooner the better!

Harry's very good for other people's health. Whenever they see him coming they go for a long walk!

She has real polish.
Only on her shoes.

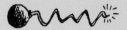

She always has an answer to every problem.
Yes, but they're always wrong.

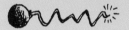

He's watching his weight.
Yes, watching it go up!

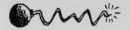

Did you here about the rub cube
for wallies?
It is yellow on all six sides.

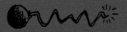

What do you call a gorilla with two
bananas in his ears?
Anything you like, because he can't
hear you.

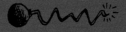

Ben: You'd be a great player if it weren't for two things.
Len: What are they?
Ben: Your feet.

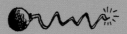

What happened when the umpire had a brain transplant?
The brain rejected him.

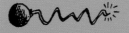

That's Wicked

After years of traveling around the world in his search, the wicked Abanazar finally discovered the enchanted cave in which he believed lay the magic lamp which would make him millions. He stood before the boulders which sealed the cave, and uttered the magic words. "Open sesame!" There was a silence, and then a ghastly voice from within moaned, "Open says-a-who?"

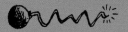

Doctor: You seem to be in good health, Mrs Brown. Your pulse is as steady and regular as clockwork.
Mrs Brown: That's because you've got your hand on my watch.

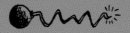

Did you hear about the good geography master?
He had abroad knowledge of his subject.

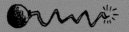

What is small, furry and wicked at sword fights?
A mouseketeer.

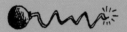

A monster went to see the doctor because he kept bumping into things. "You need glasses," said the doctor.
"Will I be able to read with them?" asked the monster.
"Yes."
"That's wicked," said the monster. I didn't know how to read before."

How do ghosts learn songs?
They read the sheet music.

At the school concert, Wee Willie
had volunteered to play his
bagpipes. The noise was dreadful,
like a choir of cats singing off-key.
After he'd blown his way through
The Flowers of the Forest he said,
"Is there anything you'd like me to
play?"
"Yes!" cried a voice from the back
of the hall. "Dominoes!"

Freda: Do you like my new hairstyle?
Freddie: It's wicked. It covers most of your face.

Jimmy: Why do you always play the same piece of music at the school concert?
Timmy: Because it haunts me.
Jimmy: I'm not surprised, you murdered it weeks ago.

Soprano at concert: And what would you like me to sing next?
Member of audience: Do you know Old Man River?
Soprano: Er, yes.
Member of audience: Well go jump in it.

A flute player was walking home late one night from a concert. He took a short cut through the local woods, and he hadn't gone far before he bumped into a ghost and then a vampire. Pulling out his flute he began to play a lovely trilling melody – the ghost and the vampire stood entranced. Soon a crowd of phantoms, monsters, goblins, cannibals and witches listening to the music, surrounded the musician. Then up bounded a werewolf. "Yum! Yum!" he growled, and gobbled up the flute player. "Why did you do that?" complained the others. "We were enjoying it."

"Eh, what was that?" said the deaf werewolf.

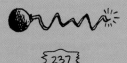

What happened when the old witch went to see a wicked film?
The manager told her to cut the cackle.

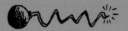

At a concert, the boring singer with the tuneless voice announced, "I should now like to sing *Over The Hills and Far Away*."
"Thank goodness for that," whispered someone in the audience. "I thought he was going to stay all evening."

Where do geologists go for
entertainment?
To rock concerts.

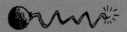

Freddie had persuaded Amanda
to marry him, and was formally
asking her father for his
permission. "Sir," he said, "I would
like to have your daughter for my
wife."
"Why can't she get one of her
own?" said Amanda's father.

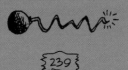

A cannibal known as Ned
Ate potato crisps in his bed.
His mother said, "Sonny, it's not
very funny
Why don't you eat people instead?"

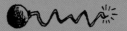

1st monster: I have a hunch.
2nd monster: I thought you were a
funny shape.

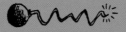

Where do spiders go for fun?
To Webley.

Witch: I got up really early this morning and opened the door in my nightie!
Wizard: That's a wicked place to keep a door.

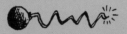

I had a wicked dream last night, Mom.
Did you?
I dreamed I was awake, but when I woke up I found I was asleep.

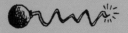

What is big, hairy and can fly
faster than sound.
King Koncord.

What did the papa ghost say to the
baby ghost.
Fasten your sheet belt.

Games mistress: Come on, Sophie.
You can run faster than that.
Sophie: I can't, miss. I'm wearing
run-resistant tights.

I Saw a Vampire – by Ron Fast

Two fleas were running across the
top of a packet of soap powder.
"Why are we running so fast?"
gasped one.
"Because it says 'Tear Along the
Dotted Line.'"

What is wet and slippery and likes
Latin American music?
A conga eel.

Why can you run faster when
you've got a cold?
Because you have a racing pulse
and a running nose.

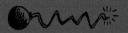

A young lad was helping his dad
with do-it-yourself jobs around
the house. "You know, son," said
the father, "you're just like
lightning with that hammer."
"Fast, eh?" said the boy.
"Oh, no – you never strike in the
same place twice."

Hil: Who was the fastest runner in history?
Bill: Adam. He was first in the human race.

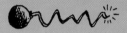

"I hope this plane doesn't travel faster than sound," said the old lady to the air stewardess.
"Why?"
"Because my friend and I want to talk, that's why."

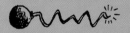

Dad, would you like to save some money?
I certainly would, son.
Any suggestions?
Sure. Why not buy me a bike, then I won't wear my shoes out so fast.

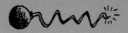

What's a skeleton's favorite musical instrument?
A trom-bone.

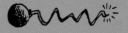

What do ghosts dance to?
Soul music.

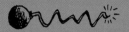

Did you hear about the musical
ghost?
He wrote haunting melodies.

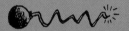

Why don't skeletons play music in
church?
They have no organs.

Music student: Did you really learn to play the violin in six easy lessons?

Music teacher: Yes, but the 500 that followed were pretty difficult.

What's yellow and fills fields with music?
Popcorn.

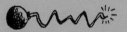

Classified advertisement: For sale. 1926 hearse. Wicked condition; original body.

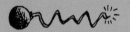

Big-headed player: I've been told I have music in my feet.
His friend: Yes, two flats!

They say music has a terrible effect on him. It makes him play his violin.

Mother: Polly is a natural cello player.
Music teacher: You mean she has bow legs?

What's a stone's favorite music?
Rock and Roll.